How to make a Present

Paul Humphrey

Photography by Chris Fairclough

W
FRANKLIN WATTS
LONDON•SYDNEY

First published in 2006 by
Franklin Watts
338 Euston Road
London NW1 3BH

Franklin Watts Australia
Hachette Children's Books
Level 17/207 Kent Street
Sydney NSW 2000

© 2006 Franklin Watts

ISBN: 0 7496 6607 2 (hbk)
ISBN: 0 7496 6857 1 (pbk)

Dewey classification number: 745.5

A CIP catalogue record for this book is available
from the British Library.

Planning and production by Discovery Books Limited
Editor: Rachel Tisdale
Designer: Ian Winton
Photography: Chris Fairclough
Series advisors: Diana Bentley MA and Dee Reid MA,
Fellows of Oxford Brookes University

The author, packager and publisher would like to thank Ottilie Austin-Baker for
her participation in this book.

Printed in China

Contents

What you need

Do you like dinosaurs? Here's how to make a dinosaur present!

These are the things you will need:

A large mixing bowl

A pencil

150g of salt

300g of flour

A wooden spoon

A table knife

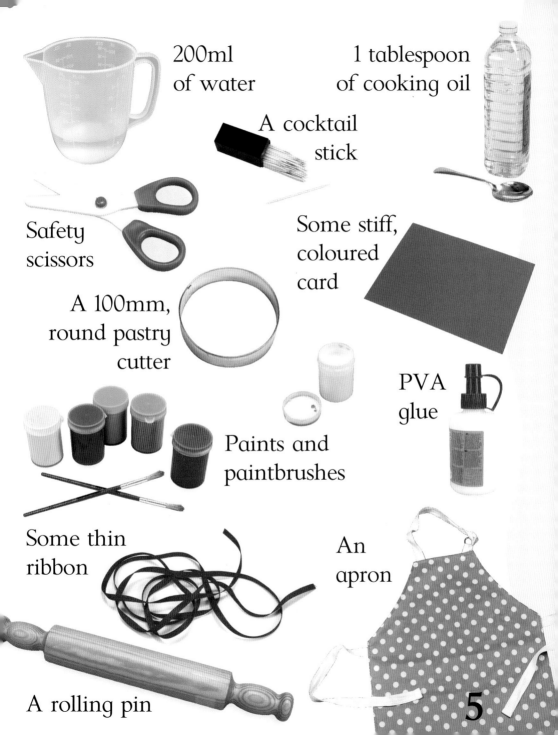

200ml of water

1 tablespoon of cooking oil

A cocktail stick

Safety scissors

Some stiff, coloured card

A 100mm, round pastry cutter

PVA glue

Paints and paintbrushes

Some thin ribbon

An apron

A rolling pin

5

Drawing the dinosaur

First, draw a dinosaur shape like this on to the card.

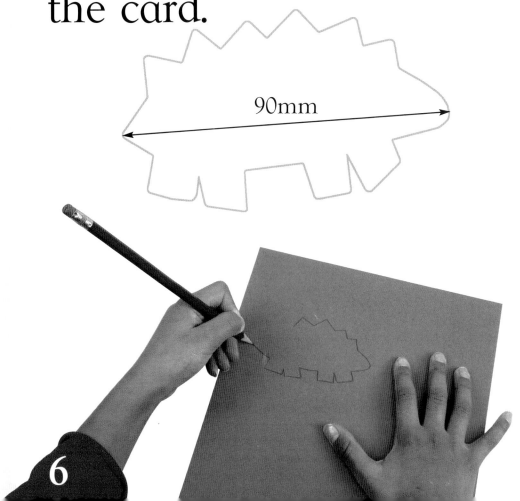

90mm

Make it 90mm from head to tail.

Carefully cut out the dinosaur shape.

Making the dough

Next, put the flour and salt into the mixing bowl, and stir.

Pour in the water a little at a time.

Add the oil.

Keep stirring the sticky mixture.

Knead the
mixture to make
a smooth
dough.

Spread some
flour over the
worktop.

Then roll out the dough
until it is about 5mm
thick.

Cutting the dough

Cut out a circle of dough.

Press the card dinosaur
onto the leftover dough
and cut around it.

Sticking the circles together

Sprinkle some water over the dough circle.

Gently press the dough
dinosaur onto the circle.

Drying your present

Use the cocktail stick to make a hole at the top of the circle.

Make a face for your dinosaur.

16

Leave your present
to dry for 2-3 days.

Or ask an adult to bake
it at 120°C (gas mark $\frac{1}{2}$)
for 8 hours.

Painting your present

When it is dry, paint your present with white paint. Leave it to dry.

Next, paint the background and the dinosaur in bright colours.

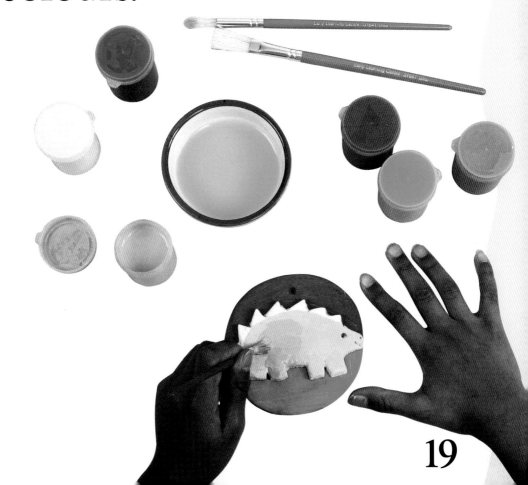

Finishing your present

When the paint is dry, brush on two coats of PVA glue.

This will stop the paint coming off your present.

Leave it to dry.

Wrapping your present

Thread the ribbon through the hole.

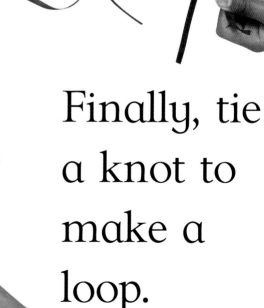

Finally, tie a knot to make a loop.

Now you can wrap your dinosaur present and give it to a friend.

Steps

Can you remember all of the steps to make your present?

1. Draw and cut out the shape.

2. Make the dough.

3. Cut the dough.

4. Press the pieces.

5. Make the face.

6. Bake the dough.

7. Paint the present.

8. Tie the ribbon.

9. Wrap the present.